The Lace of Tough Mesquite

A TEXAS HERITAGE

Winner of the 1992 William E. Bard Book Award

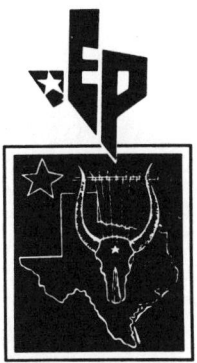

Sponsored by The Poetry Society of Texas

The Lace of Tough Mesquite

A TEXAS HERITAGE

BY
E'LANE CARLISLE MURRAY

Illustrations by Ty Heintze and Charles Shaw

EAKIN PRESS

txr

FIRST EDITION

Copyright © 1993
By E'Lane Carlisle Murray

Manufactured in the United States of America
By Eakin Press
An Imprint of Sunbelt Media, Inc.
P.O. Drawer 90159 ★ Austin, TX 78709-0159

ALL RIGHTS RESERVED. No part of this book may be reproduced in any form without written permission from the publisher, except for brief passages included in a review appearing in a newspaper or magazine.

ISBN 0-89015-903-3

Library of Congress Cataloging-in-Publication Data

Murray, E'Lane Carlisle.
   The lace of tough mesquite : a Texas heritage / E'Lane Carlisle Murray.
     p.   cm.
   ISBN 0-89015-903-3 : $12.95
   1. Texas – Poetry. I. Title.
PS3563.U767L33   1993
811'.54 – dc20   93-2915
                                                                            CIP

For Minnie Johanna

Acknowledgments

In grateful appreciation to the editors of the following publications and to The Poetry Society of Texas for their Annual Awards.

Bird Watcher's Digest: Cactus Condo; If Grasses Whisper; The Water's Tune.

ByLine Magazine: Beach Runner; Shoreline Primitive; Rainstorm; From the Pier; Wind Wake; The Gold Bar Pin; Evening Echoes; Morning Thieves.

The Christian Science Monitor: Whooping Cranes Return.

Poetry Society of Texas Annuals: White Bridge (1988); Autumn Invasion (1988); The Fence Line (1989); Passerby at Indian Point (1991); Canyon Trail (1991).

Potpourri: Rain Bird; Summer's End.

Rider: Boerne Motorcyclist.

Z Miscellaneous: Golden Straw.

Byliners Texas-Wide Writers Competition: Spring Storage (First Place Award, Rhymed Poem, 1988).

Contents

ROADSIDE HERITAGE — 1
- Roadside Heritage — 2
- The Gentle Ghosts — 3
- Georgia Arline Graves — 4
- Edward Hastings — 5
- Little Arline Hastings — 6
- Minnie Johanna — 7–9
- The Gold Bar Pin, Alma Elizabeth — 10
- Foundation, Old Bayview Cemetery — 11
- Thistle Quilt — 12
- Britches Quilt — 13
- Pedernales Pattern — 14
- Golden Straw — 15
- Where is the Spring? — 16
- Crossing the Brazos — 17
- The Fence Line — 18
- Indian Prayer Wheel — 19

A YEAR OF TEXAS SEASONS — 20
- White Bridge — 22
- Wind Wake — 23
- Garden Imprint — 24
- February's Spring — 25
- Spring Storage — 26
- Appointment with Spring — 27
- Summer's Place — 28
- Tethered — 29
- Cicadas — 30
- Summer's End — 31
- Shades of Conte Crayon — 32
- Where is Red Autumn? — 33
- Rainstorm — 34
- October Ghosts — 35
- Hill Country Thanksgiving — 36

TEXAS FLYWAY 38
   Whooping Cranes Return 40
   Blue Herons 41
   Flight Patterns 42
   Autumn Invasion 43
   The Water's Tune 44
   Cactus Condo 45
   If Grasses Whisper 46
TEXAS CANYONS, TEXAS COASTS 48
   Canyon Trail 50
   Reunion 51
   Chola Children 52
   Shoreline Primitive 53
   Port Mansfield: From the Pier 54
   Altiplanic Arrangement 55
   Rain Bird 56
   Morning Thieves 57
   Boerne Motorcyclist 58
   Evening Echoes 59
   Beach Runner 60
   Passerby at Indian Point 61

Roadside Heritage

ROADSIDE HERITAGE

Along the Interstate, in median
frames, bluebonnets nod and Indian
paintbrush flames, brushing across
the thoughts we hold inside.

Once flower carpets spread across
the wide prairies. Beneath the lace
of tough mesquite, the colors stroked
broad land — reached out to meet broad skies.

The present-past stays close beside
us on the gray asphalt. Pale shadows
ride along, unmindful of our pace.
With sudden flash, a field lark veers,
reveals a yellow splash, circling
into the windblown, roadside grass.

We hold fast to the scenes
we think we pass.

THE GENTLE GHOSTS

No broad highway leads to the sandy point
between the Copano and Saint Charles Bays,
where live oak trees and bay trees sink their roots
and yaupon hugs dim trails with scalloped leaves.

A wooden stile invites the passerby
to enter a small graveyard, and to see
stone markers naming those who once lived here —
who waded the warm tides, or huddled close
and turned their backs to cold December winds.

Positioned here, long after life was gone,
two granite stones are placed close side-by-side.
One is inscribed, "Georgia Arline," the mother —
"Little Arline" is engraved on the other.

Who comes to read these legends, names and dates?
Those who work to trace vague genealogies,
who treasure family stories often told,
and ghosts, the gentle ghosts, who come remembering,
who touch our sleeves and ask us to sit down.

GEORGIA ARLINE GRAVES
(1845 – 1886)

I laughed with Sarah as we crossed the street,
trying to keep the mud off of our shoes.
Then we looked up to see our old school marm
with a man, just new in town, from Delaware.
"Edward," I heard her say, "meet Arline Graves."

My family feared he was a Yankee spy,
coming to Texas from so far away.
We married soon and soon were on our own.
Sons and daughters came and grew, until in time
we made our home along this inland bay.

Our garden grew, green in the summer sun.
The chickens nested — left their warm brown eggs —
the gentle cows stood quiet while our pails
filled full with milk. Fish and wild game were here
and always free. And Edward had the time
for teaching lessons on his violin.

The end was near for me, my summer days.
I held my tiny August child, a girl.
I held her close and closed my eyes to see
that time long past when I was laughing as
we crossed the muddy street . . . the lovely street.

EDWARD HASTINGS
(1836 – 1929)

From Delaware I made my way and brought
my violin; I can't remember if I meant
to stay. The trees were not as tall, or green,
the rivers not as deep or broad, and yet
each Texas morning kept me here. I met
Georgia Arline in Eighteen-Sixth-Three
at Columbus on the Colorado.

Our first child came — Minnie Johanna.
We moved from place to place, our family grew.
With four farm lots we settled where gnarled live
oak trees lean with the winds from Saint Charles

Death took my wife and left "Little Arline."
Three years we loved this fragile child. Death too
her too. I left Lamar and took my violin.

LITTLE ARLINE HASTINGS
(1886 – 1889)

My sister Minnie always dressed my doll.
I hadn't learned to tie the sash in back.
She read to me from Mama's poem book . . .
the words sounded like music when she talked.

When brother Ben had chopped the kindlin' wood,
he took me out to that big live oak tree
and spread a pallet down there in the shade,
or lifted me to that low-hanging limb,
where I could watch the older children play.

When Papa came home after work was done
and everyone sat down at supper time,
he'd take his fiddle down and play for us
so we could tap our feet, and sway, and sing.

They say my Mama loved the violin.

MINNIE JOHANNA
(1864 – 1900)

As Arline Hasting's oldest child,
  I helped her care for all the younger ones.
While still a child myself, I met and married Charlie.
  We two joined hands and soon began
        to make a home where we could raise
            a family of our own.

My daughter, Mabel, said about my life,

  "My mother was a good shot.
(Our home was on the coast
  where Papa worked at building boats.)
Mama would walk along the bay into the reeds,
        aim at the ducks that flew,
            and bring them down.

"One morning as a duck flew past
  she took dead aim, but from nearby
  a shot rang out and her bird fell.
'Mr. Smith!' she called, 'Mr. Smith!
  You shot my duck!'

"And turkeys . . .

"At dusk, wild turkeys, flying in to roost,
lined up along the railing of the fence and Mama
  lifted up her gun.
She sighted down the line and fired.
  Some turkeys flew, but seven flapped
along the fence. And Mama — clapped her hands and
  danced across the yard!
We had a feast, shared our good fortune
        with other families living near."

My daughter Alma smiled.

  "Remember how the chickens made soft clucking sounds
  and followed Mama as she walked across the yard?

    And how she always sang while cleaning house?
What were those words?
        'Scatter seeds of kindness.'
I still can hear her voice."

    I taught my girls to sweep our wooden floors.
"Just swing the broom," I said,
    "from right to left. Then stop and tack.
Just turn and sweep the other way
    till all the dust and sand is swept outside."

A fever came.
    Charlie had gone to work in Goliad.
        I wrote to him,
"It seems that someone here dies every day."

So little time to raise my brood . . .
    my seven daughters . . .
        my one son.

Our baby daughter died,
    our little Ruth, then
three dark days and I died too.

My children, whom I left so suddenly,
    cared for each other,
        followed their dreams,
            remembered how we lived
along the Saint Charles Bay and Copano,
    and how to sweep the floor.

Grandchildren never took my hand.
They only know the stories they are told.

Just swing the broom from right to left,
    then stop and tack.

Now, all the dust
    and all the sand is gone.

THE GOLD BAR PIN
ALMA ELIZABETH (1892 – 1979)

The sunlight filtered through the live oak tree,
spreading its dappled shadows on the ground.
She shook a pallet wide and let it fall
and sat down, listening to the wind's low sound.
Her hair shone smooth and dark against her skin
and, near the part, she wore a gold bar pin.

The salty tide lapped on the melting sand,
splashing the scattered shells there on the shore.
She felt the damp beach, cool beneath her feet,
and watched the sea gulls spread their wings and soar.
Her hair shone smooth and gray against her skin
and, near the part, she wore a gold bar pin.

Today, the sunlight warms the live oak tree.
The tide still moves along the sandy shore.
There by the well-worn path, she walks again,
making damp footprints, as she did before.
Her hair shines smooth and white against her skin
and, near the part, she wears a gold bar pin.

FOUNDATION
Old Bayview Cemetery

Here on this gentle hill near freeway lanes,
old monuments seem scattered on he lawn
and spectral trees spread aging fingers wide
to touch an ink black sky. The quiet here
is louder than the traffic's constant sound
as trucks and cars traverse a curved gray band.

The world's turned inside out from where they lie —
the seamen, settlers, soldiers of years past
whose names and dates, inscribed on chosen stones,
blend census with angelic art.

                                              Beyond
the sparse and windswept grass, strange monoliths
rise, grid by grid, through strips of open space.
Lights shine like structured eyes, row after row,
piercing the dark across broad freeway lanes,
bridging the cement gulf of then and now.

Towers, erected from white lines on blue,
and held in place by concrete slabs and beams,
reach toward the changing clouds. They view their
base —

the scattered stones with chisled dates, guarding
the sparse and windswept grass that covers
Old Bayview.

THISTLE QUILT

This quilt was made in Eighteen Forty-Three:
Nine thistles flaming red above green leaves,
Set off on creamy squares and framed with strips
Of that same reddish hue. Fine stitches trace
The strength of its design.

Elizabeth, Sam Houston's sister, set
Each bloom in place, somewhere in Texas or
In Tennessee, to be a wedding gift
For Cousin Sterling Houston and his bride.
The couple took the quilt with them to Bend
In Texas on San Saba County's line.
There Martha shook it wide across the bed,
Bright as the fire that crackled on the hearth.

When raiding Indians wandered on the trails,
Along the Colorado River banks,
The treasured quilt was folded, packed inside
A lard can, buried underneath a tree.

Five years passed by and brought a safer time,
A time for digging deep and to reclaim.

Now on display — it's spread across the wall,
Its printed legend tacked inside it there.
The thistles flame, still red, but gently grayed:
Their sign and seal of unforgotten times.

BRITCHES QUILT

While chill drafts found the narrow chinks
And squeezed with frigid force inside,
Small children snuggled in a quilt
Made of cloth strips — four inches wide.

Strips cut from britches with worn knees —
Some of them brown, some gray, some black,
Salvaged from close along the seams
And held in place with quilting tack.

The pattern was unplanned but, like
Plowed fields, took on each hidden hue
Of the raw earth. There in its warmth,
While winds blew cold, the children grew.

PEDERNALES PATTERN

Miss Callie's pieced herself a patchwork quilt
to spread across the bed in her spare room.
It's colored like the cedar-dotted hills
and touched with tints of sage's purple bloom.

Fine stitches hold each pattern in its place:
a curving strip of Pedernales green
with clumps of Indian blanket near the banks
to add their reds and yellows to the scene.

With chimneys made of native limestone blocks,
a dogtrot house, with a wide porch for shade,
a windmill, and a live oak tree are placed
on gingham squares that Callie's scissors made.

High on the thermal drafts, a buzzard soars.
A goat stands balanced on a barren ledge.
Along the fence, a paisano runs
into a spiny agarita hedge.

The needle gleams and pulls the matching thread
to tack the desert candles' skyward tilt,
while neighbors come to bring the latest news
and brag on Callie's Pedernales quilt.

GOLDEN STRAW

I walk along the weed-grown path
to the chicken house
old and weathered now.

The door squeaks a loud complaint
as I stoop forward
and go inside —

the nests are empty
boxes now
with bits of dusty straw.

Not along ago, it seems,
the straw was fresh and golden
and, setting there, the fluffed-up hens
made curious clucking sounds
when I walked in,
White Leghorns
Plymouth Rocks
Rhode Island Reds.

They guarded smooth warm eggs,
some white, some brown.
They scolded, questioned me
with round indignant eyes.

I remember, and they are gone.

The door squeaks loudly as I leave
and echoes as I walk away.

The sunlight touches
a bit of golden straw.

WHERE IS THE SPRING?

Uncle Charlie took us there   Dad
and me   through a grove of young sycamores
shafts of sunlight sliding through
the leaves   Near a spring gushing with
air bubbles   I sat on the grass   Lichen
on damp gray rocks made a paisley
pattern and water formed a clear
green path   I was part of its flowing
its whispering

Brother voices of Dad and Uncle Charlie
blended with the sounds   leaves   water
They laughed and their gray-blue eyes
crinkled at the corners   What are they
remembering   I wondered and threw a smooth
gray stone in the water

Uncle Charlie seemed a part of the woodland
close-cropped hair   steel-gray   reflecting
sunlight   His face showed brown   lined
like a woodcarving   standing with one foot
on a fallen log   I remember him that way

Deep in my pocket I slipped a stone
Someday   I'll come back here
         to this same spring
I've looked but where I thought it flowed
only a trickle of water cuts through dusty
         rocks   Is this the place?
Where? I should have asked Uncle Charlie
but he is gone   he and the spring

Somewhere   by a grove of old sycamores
shafts of sunlight sliding through
the leaves   the spring gushes   foams
a clear green path   I listen for its
whispering   look for its flowing
I touch the smooth gray stone

CROSSING THE BRAZOS

We traveled south from Dallas, Dad and I.
driving a new sedan, a dark blue Nash.
The narrow roads were not like freeways now.

Each hill we crested brought us some new sight:
Yellow fields of coreopsis rippled
in the wind — row after row of cotton,
dark green ins summer's sun, and corn grew tall
with silken tassels shining on each ear.
A farmhouse, where blue maypops climbed the fence,
had arborvitaes by the wooden steps.
From shaded porches, barefoot children waved.

Near Waco, as the road made a wide curve
and slanted downward toward the bottom land,
we saw a bridge. Its steel framework stood out
between tall elms and dancing cottonwoods,
reached wide from bank to bank, a giddy span.

"There's the muddy old Brazos River!" Dad
intoned and made me wonder who had known
the winding, broad, brick-colored stream before.

As we crossed over, high among the trees,
I watched the whirlpools chase each other out
of sight and we drove on to crest another hill.

The road we traveled on is hidden now.
Divided highways carry vans and cars,
but where the muddy Brazos holds its course,
the legends, lore, and tales of other days
still swirl beneath the elms and cottonwoods.

THE FENCE LINE

At the top of the rise,
the rider drew rein
and saw stretched before him
a brush-studded plain.

The soft desert wind
blew the cedar's fresh smell
as his horse stepped with care,
down the steep rocky trail.

At the foot of the hill,
he shifted his weight
and the hoofs of his horse
built a fast steady gait.

Behind him the dust rose.
He pounded a track
till his eyes saw a fence line,
narrow and black.

At the sight of the dark strand
he changed his straight course
and veered toward the open
and challenged his horse.

Away into nowhere,
away in a streak,
sweat staining his shoulders
dust streaking his cheek.

INDIAN PRAYER WHEEL

Great Spirit
moving on the burnished sky
whispering winds

We watch in silence as you hover
breathing clouds

Bring us soft rain
full ears of corn
much game   wild honey

Bring us streams   singing
deep lakes reflecting blue
or cloud-touched green

Weave for us the rainbow
soft colored path
spectrum of dreams
of promise

Stain on each brow the mystic mark
strong son   spirit soft as mist
creator

Send to these plains
the unexpected gift
widen our eyes
cause whispered songs
drum beats   drum beats

Send to these plains
the unexpected gift

White Buffalo   White Buffalo

A Year of Texas Seasons

WHITE BRIDGE

Warmth is only where my chin digs deep
into its knitted resting place.

The world is white on white:
a cold moon drifts above white birches
that sway and glisten in the wind.
Iced hedges huddle close
against white walls.
Adrift in snow,
the wide white fields become the sky.

In minor key, the wind spreads wide
then mounts a higher scale.
A sudden sweep blows spears of ice.
Surrounded, stung by driven
snow, I find no path
to follow to White Bridge.

My cold white footprints
follow me.

WIND WAKE

The barren branches scraped across the roof
as January's wind tore at the trees
and whirling in a circle through the yard
it swept along a swirl of russet leaves.

Awakened by the fury of the sound,
she rose to make a banging door shut fast
and feeling all the winter's icy chill
her shoulders tensed against a bitter blast.

A cold white moon hung brilliant in the sky,
lighting the patterned tiles outside the door.
She tightly pushed the latch and darkness fell
across the old hooked rug there on the floor.

GARDEN IMPRINT

She knelt and placed the bulbs on loosened ground,
In her hand a weathered trowel with crooked blade.
She dug a row of holes, pushed back each mound,
Sprinkling bonemeal in each dip she made.
In shallow beds she dropped the dry brown corms,
Seeing the colors — yellows, blues, and reds,
And with sandy loam she covered dormant forms,
Smoothing dirt like blankets on their beds.
The ground felt hard and damp beneath her knees.
She crumpled tight the bonemeal's empty sack.
Above she saw bright sky between the trees
Where branches laced the blue with winter's black.
Beneath her agile fingers, the damp clays
Retained the lasting imprint of her ways.

FEBRUARY'S SPRING

The window frames the ivory-blossomed pear
of this gray spring   I lift my cup to taste
the steaming tea and wrap myself in sweet

                remembering

The heart-shaped box   the chocolate creams,
dark diamonds, ovals, squares   each in a
fluted paper cup   and filled with unexpected
nuts   or candied fruit

                remembering

The bright bouquets   the tulip's flame
and purple iris — yellow throated —
airy sprigs of baby's breath   cool
in a cone of paper lace   these amulets
red satin charms of February's spring

                remembering

The pear tree nods   I tip my empty cup
drained of the last sweet steaming drop

But you are here   you touch my hand
                and fill my cup again.

SPRING STORAGE
(For Shane)

We kneel there side by side and pull the weeds
Then break the hardened clods of dirt and clay.
His fingers draw straight furrows for dark seeds;
I crumble bonemeal, dry and dusty gray.
Along each row we drop the jet-black beads
That soon will burst and make a bright bouquet.
Our heads are bowed beneath the sun's warm light.
His blond hair shines, while mine shows streaks of white.

Grandson and I sit down against the trees
Looking back, on fresh turned flower beds,
While from some apiary, golden bees
Glide through the tasseled branches near our heads.
With leaf, and cloud, and blue-sky canopies,
Woven with shade, and sunlight's yellow threads,
We store the sight, the sound, the feel of spring,
To keep this day for our remembering.

APPOINTMENT WITH SPRING

The redbud blooms when spring is bleak and chill.
Its blossoms range from pink to deepest rose,
Sending a blush across the barren hill.
Here, on a slanting ridge, while soft wind blows,
I stop, to catch my breath, where redbud glows.
I hear a whispered sound, sudden and slight:
The whistling wings of doves in startled flight.

Soft doves who skim the trail, the dormant grass,
And punctuate the morning's gentle gray,
Your flight is mine. With you I swiftly pass
The reach of flower-covered limbs that sway,
Drawn to this hillside where I cannot stay.
I promise hillside spirits, hovering near,
Just like the redbud, I'll return next year.

SUMMER'S PLACE

Above the broad stream's softly singing falls,
sunlight breaks through a canopy of leaves,
touching the vines that trail along the bank.
I walk a narrow path that twists and weaves
to reach fresh clumps of mint and river fern,
and by the shallows, watch swift currents churn.

Wading into the water, ankle deep,
where breezes tangle wisps of loosened hair,
I see a flash of iridescent sheen —
a pair of dragonflies pause in the air.
While warblers ride arpeggios overhead,
I splash along the creek's smooth limestone bed.

Each summer I return to this clear stream,
laughing to see its winding path once more,
as if it clings to every rocky curve,
retracing ripples pushed onto the shore.
There in the water I can see my face,
unfocused, but secure in summer's place.

TETHERED

The sun strings lights across the clear blue lake
While willows dip green leaves along its banks.
My boat slips quietly in, nudging the pier,
And I step out to stand on weathered planks.

The shaded waters lap beneath the pier,
Moving in toward my deck chair on the sand.
I take a cold drink from a styrofoam chest
While melting ice drops from my sunburned hand.

Bright sun reflects its glare across my view,
Closing my eyes, but leaving me awake.
Time slows its beat in summer's golden haze.
The tethered boat and I float with the lake.

CICADAS

Day at its beginning
streaks light across the sky.
In the early stillness,
the shrill cicadas cry.
July's heat has willed them
from the grass into the trees,
crawling green, throbbing brown,
monopolizing miles of sound.
Their meter never hesitates
in fear of their monotony
but, pulsing with insistent beat,
pervades the summer's mounting heat.
Their mesmerizing wild sweet cry
breaks with a punctuated clack
then builds until the sound is back.

Then, when their cry is gone at last,
dry shells of silence dot the grass.

SUMMER'S END

The water in our hands was clear and blue
We spread our fingers wide and it slipped through.

While easy laughter rang across the park,
Our tender skin turned to a summer brown.
We dived into the pool where golden lights
Reflected as the blue depths led us down.

At summer's end, we raced the metered lanes,
Then shook clear drops of water from our hair.
We tracked the empty sidewalk with wet feet
And calling, "See you," left faint echoes there.

Gone is the summer, gone the quick goodbye,
Gone are the footprints that we left to dry.
The water in our hands was clear and blue —
We spread our fingers wide and love slipped through.

SHADES OF CONTE CRAYON

A copper sun projects pink light
across the distant range where ancient
wanderers built campfires in the night
Sandia Mountain —
rising from forever.

Soft shadows fall below a tree's bare
limbs, while strange winds whisper.
Once beneath thick leaves, now withered,
the wanderers rested.

Chants of moons long-past
echo from the Old Town Plaza where
conte crayon tribes fashion
silver jewels and, with strong fingers,
set smooth stones, fallen
from a turquoise sky.

Conte crayon shades cling to
distant mountains, to gaunt old trees,
to faces lined with legends, and
to my fingers — touching them with
mystic chalk.

WHERE IS RED AUTUMN?

The signature of autumn always seems
to top the mountains in a swirl of red
and drop a widening line of yellow-gold
in downward spirals to broad river banks.

Here on warm coastal plains, we strive to find
some whispered note that signals
falls arrival.

Where is red autumn when green summer stays?

At times it hovers in a blue-black sky
and, while we watch, sends chilling
winds that lift sparse tallow leaves
like yellow birds in flight.

At times it makes the golden rain tree bow
as if to welcome to a fall buffet
the migrant warblers darting quickly past.

Always, the curving bay turns turquoise green
and constant waves are topped with frosted curls.

Buoyant, it floats between the heat and cold,
uncertain of the better choice, to splash
along the beach's warm wet sand, or chase
the swift gray squirrel with icy blasts —
    it waits.

Autumn, I know you well
although you veil your face. I touch your
braille-like signature and crunch brown leaves
beneath my walking shoes. I feel your whispered
song. I whisper too.
Autumn, you know me well.

RAINSTORM

The raindrops make small fountains at my feet
And swaying trees bend low along the street.
Wet pavement shows the headlights' yellow gleam;
Tires sizzle on the dark road's shallow stream.
Each splashing step sounds hollow as I rush
To leap the curb where churning waters gush.

Running along the walk, I reach our door
And, inside, kick my shoes off on the floor.
I make a pot of tea and feel the steam,
Then in my cup stir sugar and some cream.
I listen to the wind and pounding rain
Then draw the curtain back, to look again.

OCTOBER GHOSTS

October morning brings a cool foretaste
Of windblown hours too few and sweet to waste.
Choosing a day to gather on the coast,
We seek to honor each elusive ghost
Whose granite marker on the site is placed.

In staggered rows, the aging graves are traced
Beneath live oaks with branches interlaced —
Are marked with dates and names we treasure most.
       October morning.

We climb a wooden stile. Our steps, slow paced,
Descend where family members now have faced
A printed sign of caution on a post,
"Please close the gate securely or the most
Of our elusive ghosts may leave with haste."
       October morning.

HILL COUNTRY THANKSGIVING

For streaks of sunlight on the fence
That changes night to day,
For early morning frost that steams
And deer that bound away,
We offer bounteous thanks,

For cactus clumps along the trail
Beneath sprawling mesquite,
For wild turkey who track the sand
With cryptographic feet,
We offer bounteous thanks.

For family members, old and new,
With growing appetites
Whose warm eyes laugh as they reflect
The oak logs' snapping lights,
We offer bounteous thanks.

For cranberries that boil and pop,
For tastes with stirring-spoon,
For reassuring promises,
"It will be ready soon."
We offer bounteous thanks.

Around the table we join hands
And bow our heads to say,
"The hill country has filled our hearts
On this Thanksgiving Day."
We offer bounteous thanks.

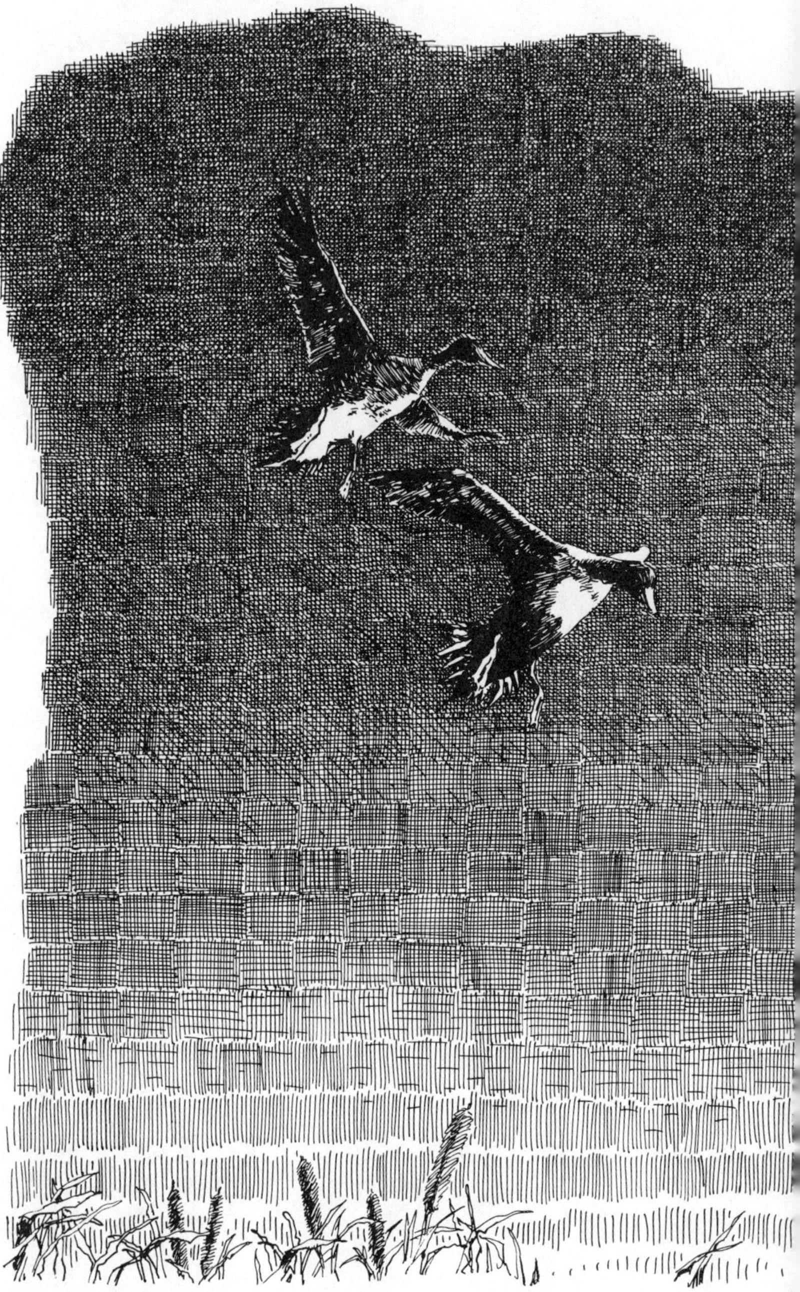

Texas Flyway

WHOOPING CRANES RETURN

Autumn clouds streak low across the sky
and waves splash on the island shore,
while whooping cranes fly in like kites
along Aransas Bay. Banking broad wings,
they touch down on the dunes.

With russet fledgling and a constant mate,
each pair stakes boundaries near the
blackjack oaks,
returning always to the site once claimed.

In bronze sea oats they stretch and preen,
white feathers gleaming in the sun.
They stride on black stilt legs across
the flats into the tide.
Topaz eyes search for blue crabs that scuttle
sideways past their feet.

At alien sounds, they lift their heads,
flashing scarlet caps, black masks, and amber
beaks. "Ker-loo," they bugle,
"ker-lee-oo."
Black-tipped wings spread wide to rise,
to glide high on the wind.
Great shadows skim the sand.

Endangered beauty free and unaware that once
their flock was almost gone, that watchful
boaters in tall grass along the waterline
are numbering them with quiet applause,
cheering their growing autumn flight
above Aransas Bay.

BLUE HERONS

Along the hillside where I drove,
a pair of herons lifted high,
crossing above me on the wind,
with blue-gray wings against the sky.

I watched them glide and fade from sight,
straining to see them as before.
On blue-gray wings against the sky,
they left me by the roadside shore.

Their shadows floated on the tide,
as strong wings moved in symmetry,
soaring to reach the silver line,
where heaven slips into the sea.

FLIGHT PATTERNS

Chill Autumn hovers dark
across the bay and riding
on a sweep of upper air
a skein of snow geese honk

to one another, and the world.
We lift our hands and point,
"Look, there they are!"
The line is black, now silver,
in the sun. The slow warm

cast of summer days is gone,
and quickening pulses beat
with those strong wings

that push against the morning
sky, and with their pattern
      signal change:

change for the snow geese,
change for me.

AUTUMN INVASION

At dusk we are invaded
by winged hummers, flying low.
Green jewels gleam above
the velvet lawn,
crisscrossing their own paths.
There where wide scarlet blooms unfold,
small great warriors stake their space.

They hover, draw back, and shoot upward
until, lost among thick leaves,
we hear their cryptic signals
whispered overhead.

A sudden foray, and they drop
like feathered armies from the trees.
Whirring gauze wings, they gleam
green gold, then swirl away:
bright migrants, ghosts, or wandering
angels.

THE WATER'S TUNE

I cross the wooden footbridge where the rain
has filled a dry arroyo with a stream
that rushes toward the wide and shallow bay.
I close my eyes to hear the water's tune.

Like alien statues, great blue herons stand
among dense clumps of bluestem. Along the
bank, a young night-heron hides, and widgeon
ducks and mallards circle channels near
the cat-tail reeds. Three mud-hens paddle by.

The boardwalk cuts the sandy marsh in half
and, at its end, keen birders search the bay.
Binoculars reach past the black-necked stilts
and focus on a piling-perch where, like
some clown in red yarn wig, an egret scans
the salty bay — a reddish egret, brought
so close, I see the tousled feather top,
sharp pointed bill, and piercing eyes.

                              Time drifts
until, again, I pass the mud-hens and
the young night-heron on its branch. I see
the footbridge where the rain-stream cuts its path
and rushes toward the wide and shallow bay.

I close my eyes to keep the water's tune.

CACTUS CONDO

The jaunty pyrrhuloxias fly in,
perch high up on the prickly pear's top deck.
Flaunting pert scarlet caps,
they cock their heads.

The ground floor occupants are neat bobwhites
who, in a line, sail out like feathered skiffs
among gold seas of ripening prairie grass.

Wild turkeys land with iridescent sheen
and strut across the tarmac with a twist
of red sinewy necks. Cactus condo
safe refuge, meeting place,
brush country hub.

IF GRASSES WHISPER
(Hans Suter Park)

Near roads
    that carry traffic into town
with black-barred wings
    white pelicans fly in
to glide like feathered boats on Oso Bay
Above the shallow flats
    a wooden walk leads
upward to a bank of natural growth
mesquite
        granjeno
                huisache
                      prickly pear

In warm southeastern winds
    lithe grasses dip with
golden seed heads glinting in the sun
Deep   in thick bluestem clumps   nest
native birds
Rabbits scurry   small insects creep
    and fly
leaf-cutter ants
        wolf spiders
            paper wasps

Such primal ground   made safe from urban
    spread   applauds its keepers
as if grasses whisper
    where else   where else
        The world is rooted here

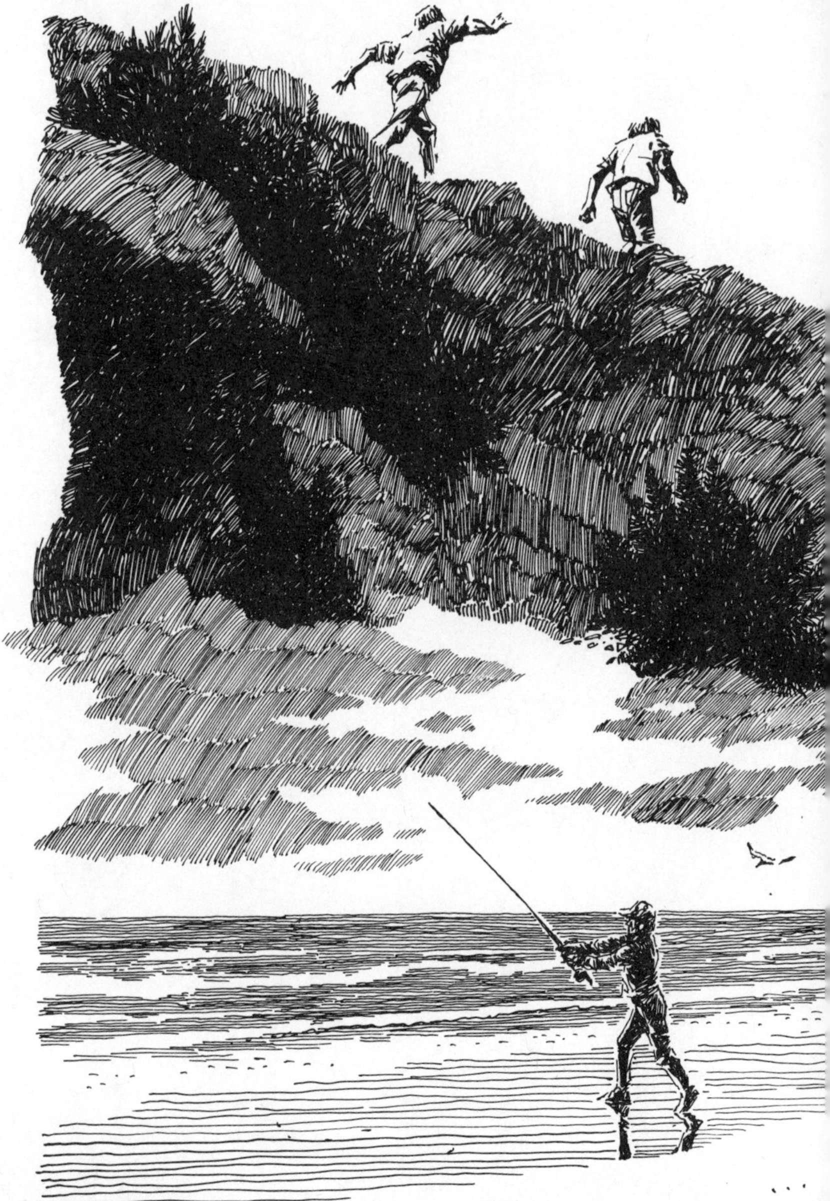

Texas Canyons, Texas Coasts

CANYON TRAIL

Between the canyon walls, the wind
plays red-gold leaves like
tissue castanets.

Along the rushing stream, a bright
leaf rides the foam, whirling into a quiet
cove, to float and fade.

I climb against the wind, crossing
a dip on wide spaced stones. In the shelter
of a deep green cedar's shade, I pause
and knot my shoestrings tight.

The crooked trail winds up
to a rock ledge where autumn spreads
a jeweled skirt: topaz, garnet, jade.

I hold the canyon's color;
its gray rocks hold me.

REUNION

We took our childhood days
and shook them free
of creases packed there years before.

The four of us trudged
up an alpine slope
with collars pulled in close
about our cheeks.

Brothers and I,
bonded by other days and years,
as if no time had intervened —

the echo
as the back door slammed
and our bare feet ran fast
along the grass-rimmed path,
waded the shallow stream
where minnows darted ankle high,
and ripples soaked the rolled-up
cuffs of worn blue jeans.

Now, golden shadows of the sun
brush pastel lights across the snow,
while icy flakes spice thin, chill air,
touching our faces and our hair.

No clock, no time, no curfew hour,
just four of us together now,
and long ago.

CHOLA CHILDREN

I like your hats —
white and flat-topped, flat-brimmed,
and circled with black bands.

You face Andean mountains
so, from behind,
I see your cherub cheeks, black hair,
and fine ear-loops.

Plump square hands
    have draped a twisted scarf
    have smoothed the woolen skirts.

Plump square feet
    follow stone-paved mountain roads
    that disappear as silent snakes
    into the mist.

Do you laugh when leaves rustle
    when lakes ripple
    when winds whisper?

Chola children, with round cherub cheeks,
    listen. A mountain flute
    incants a mystic spell.

Please, turn toward me,
    I like your hats!

SHORELINE PRIMITIVE

On a smoothly painted clear blue sky,
white cotton clouds are pasted high
and scalloped waves lap on the sand,
where palm trees,
like green pin-wheels stand.

The asphalt road winds round the bay,
striped with deep yellow on dark gray,
and following its ribboned curves,
on bright chrome wheels,
a red car swerves.

Small boats bob along the docks
near beige motels of building blocks.
In white swim suits, tan figures stand
and cast dark shadows on the sand.

The sea gulls soar in graceful Vs
against blue skies, above blue seas.

PORT MANSFIELD: FROM THE PIER

The fisherman steps out and shuts the door
as slender bars of gold show in the sky
and heavy grayness hugs the curving shore.

He sees the satin water moving by
and hears it plop and surge beneath the pier
while overhead the plaintive sea gulls cry.

The water's rim reveals the sun's red sphere
that sends a streak of bronze across the bay
and suddenly the morning air is clear.

His weathered face reflects the golden day
as casting out he hears the line's shrill song
and sinker plopping in the waterway.

The undercurrent draws his bait along.
He hooks and pulls the twisting silver trout
and makes his catch before the wind grows strong.

ALTIPLANIC ARRANGEMENT

An unseen lamp spreads burnished gold
behind the charcoal mountain range
touches the village church   its finial
cross   its broad white-stuccoed walls

The gold spills over   lights the dusty
hard-packed earth   where vendors gather
side-by-side   to kneel   arrange the
produce of the land   potatoes   peppers
beans   arrange the products of their hands
the woven cloth   the baskets and clay pots

Beside the makeshift stalls   with coverings
staked wide like starched white coronettes
families   wander in and out   dotting
the golden wash like palette daubs

The vendors cluster near the church   close
as a gathering of nuns   Daughters of Charity
chaste beneath their white-winged coronettes
they bless the people   bless the land
each home   each terra cotta roof

Here on this altiplanic site   an unseen lamp
arranges burnished gold

RAIN BIRD

I celebrate the large up-turned
clay pot   its Norfolk pine sprawled
in the iris bed   while wind and rain
test fences with their force

I celebrate the broad clear window
glass   its easel spread to blend
each shade of green   each muddy
puddle deepening on the walk

And now comes darkness   starless
filled with the rain's hypnotic beat
then   cool white sheets

What unseen bird would choose to
warble in the night   I hold my
breath to hear each subtle sculptured
note   I celebrate the rain
the night   the hidden bird

MORNING THIEVES

All morning hummingbirds have dived
with shrill-soft cries.
They soar, then perch
to syphon syrup from a tube
suspended at my window.

They pierce the plastic yellow blooms
with slender bills, fly backwards,
then ascend in group pursuit — six
at one time — there must be more,
they go so fast.

My yellow pencil stops
suspended by their flight. The prose
I planned to capture on the page
has slipped away. I cannot chance
missing the sight of feathered bombers
in metallic green, or rufous hue.

Thieves, small brazen thieves:
I watch you steal my syrup
and my time.

BOERNE MOTORCYCLIST

He zips his jacket as he checks a map
marked with a route of little-traveled roads
that lead into the mountains of Virginia
by way of Tennessee and Arkansas.

He rolls his cycle forward, sets his helmet.
His motor warms at half-choke for awhile,
then thunders out onto the asphalt ribbon,
that winds between the limestone Texas hills.
He'll cross the Cibolo at Boerne,
beneath a stretch of clear October skies.

Along the river road into the Smokies
through Cherokee, onto the Blue Ridge Trail,
his camera will frame the red-gold mountains
from shaded valleys to the highest peaks.

Dusk will bring shy deer to the road's edge
where floating mist reflects his beam of light.
Somewhere, along the shores of the Potomac,
he'll stop and mark the route for his return.

At sunup, when he finds a small-town diner,
he'll sit down with the people who come in
to joke about their health, the crops, the weather
and ask him where he's heading when he leaves.

Again, he sees the gray-green limestone hills
where muted colors replace red and gold.
Gaunt mesquite trees signal by the roadway,
and home's in sight beyond the rocky draw.

EVENING ECHOES

The door behind me shuts, making a solid sound.
Outside, along the sidewalk I can smell
the fresh-cut grass and wet cement
where water trickles down the drive.

Red floribundas gleam against a smooth
green lawn. Beside the curb, a discarded
paper cup rolls in the wind, making
a hollow sound.

Joggers pass with a measured pace and, nodding,
quickly move beyond and out of sight.

Across the bay lights twinkle.
The city skyline shows against cloud banks
that gather where a red sun sets.

Evening comes with a softening light.
I circle back and reach my cement drive,

"I'm home."

       Inside,
my words re-echo through the empty house.

The door behind me shuts,
making a hollow sound.

BEACH RUNNER

The water swirled and dashed against the rocks,
tossing the white spray fiercely toward the sky.
A sea gull swirled, to rise into the gale,
and pierced the rolling cloud-bank with a cry.

Across the sky, the lightning shot in streaks,
and drums of thunder pounded through the air.
The waves built high and broke with a deep roar
and washed the sand and left the beaches bare.

Along the melting shore, a figure ran,
fleeing the slanted sheets of stinging rain,
then falling in a gut of washed-out sand,
jumped to his feet to trace the shore again.

PASSERBY AT INDIAN POINT

Here in transparent waves
that fold and seal themselves
with foam, the broken pier bows
stiffly but retains
its water-weathered grace,
accenting tides that push
and sway its

snaggled form.
Once fishermen, in boots or
canvas shoes, stood balanced
on its sturdy deck to cast
their lines. Now

where the soft roar has no final note,
now where the fine spray
smells of pungent salt,

the windblown passerby at Indian Point
is bonded with transparent waves
and broken pier.

About the Author

E'LANE CARLISLE MURRAY, daughter of Alma and Jennings Carlisle, was born in Victoria, Texas. She spent her early childhood in a number of Texas towns including Waxahachie and Dallas. In San Antonio, she graduated from Thomas Jefferson High School and attended Trinity University where she worked as assistant to history professor, Dr. Frances Kellam Hendricks.

In 1952, she and her husband, Howard Murray, moved to Corpus Christi with their three children, Dale, Michael, and Robin. She worked as parish secretary at the Episcopal Church of the Good Shepherd and resigned in 1980 to pursue her interest in writing.

She became a member of the Clara Driscoll Chapter of the Daughters of the Republic of Texas, The Byliners of Corpus Christi, The Woman's Monday Club, and The Poetry Society of Texas.

Her prose appears in *Southern Living, Corpus Christi Monthly, South Texas Informer and Business Journal,* and *Writer's Digest.* Her essays appear frequently in the *Corpus Christi Caller-Times.*

In addition to the acknowledgments listed with *The Lace of Tough Mesquite, Children's Playmate, Country Woman, Grit, Modern Maturity,* and *Ideals* have published her poetry and her name is listed in the Directory of American Poets and Fiction Writers. Corpus Christi's Central Library displayed forty of her poems during the month of August 1991.

She thanks Dr. Frank Goodwyn, former columnist for *ByLine* magazine, for his instruction and guidance and John Gunter, English professor at Del Mar Junior College, for encouraging her to write poems depicting her Lamar Peninsula ancestors.

The Lace of Tough Mesquite won the 1992 William E. Bard Memorial Book Award sponsored by Eakin Press and The Poetry Society of Texas.

HOUSTON PUBLIC LIBRARY

R01012 69628

DATE DUE			

txr

T
811
M981

MURRAY, E'LANE CARLISLE
THE LACE OF TOUGH MESQUITE
: A TEXAS HERITAGE